The Art of
COOKIES

Fast and Fun Cookie Decoration

NOGA HITRON & NATASHA HAIMOVICH
Photography by Josef Salis

TEN SPEED PRESS
Berkeley | Toronto

Copyright © 2004 by Penn Publishing Ltd.

A Kirsty Melville Book

Ten Speed Press
Box 7123
Berkeley, California 94707
www.tenspeed.com

Distributed in Australia by Simon and Schuster Australia, in Canada by Ten Speed Press Canada, in New Zealand by Southern Publishers Group, in South Africa by Real Books, and in the United Kingdom and Europe by Airlift Book Company.

Cover and text design by Michel Opatowski

Library of Congress Cataloging-in-Publication Data
Hitron, Noga.
The art of cookies : fast and fun cookie decoration / Noga Hitron and Natasha Haimovich.
p. cm.
"A Kirsty Melville Book."
Includes index.
ISBN 1-58008-632-2 (pbk.)
1. Cookies. 2. Garnishes (Cookery). I. Haimovich, Natasha. II. Title.
TX772.H555 2004
641.8'654—dc22   2004008785

Printed in Hong Kong
First printing, 2004

1 2 3 4 5 6 7 8 9 10 — 08 07 06 05 04

contents

Welcome to the world of cookie art—cookie decorating like you've never known it before. We've all seen gingerbread men, simple Christmas trees, or even Easter bunny cookies. But what about a high heel, a baseball shirt, or a colorful dragonfly cookie? What about a four-tiered wedding cake cookie? *The Art of Cookies* includes gorgeous, original designs for all these cookies and so much more.

Were you ever stuck for an original gift to give out as a party favor? Are you tired of handing out cookies with the same old designs at Halloween and Christmas? These decorated cookies are the perfect solution. Organized by theme, the stylish designs are explained with straightforward, step-by-step instructions. Every design comes with a traceable pattern to create a stencil, and photographs are included throughout to help the home cookie decorator replicate exactly what is shown in the book.

Whether you are a budding artist just waiting to let your creative juices flow or someone who loves to bake and wants to get original, this book is for you. *The Art of Cookies* will help you learn a time-honored craft in a whole new way.

introduction

cookies

the cookie recipes used for decorating produce an especially firm, flat, crumbly cookie that does not lose its shape during baking. If not using the dough right away, wrap it in plastic wrap and store it in the refrigerator for up to 1 week. Remove it from the refrigerator 3 hours before baking.

For all of the cookie shapes in this book, you will find a pattern in Cookie Patterns (page 104). Follow the instructions there for preparing your stencils.

Using stencils: Roll out the dough according to the directions for the cookie you are making. Place the stencil on top of the dough and trace the shape of the cookie using the tip of an X-acto knife or small paring knife. Remove the stencil and cut all the way through the dough with the knife. After cutting from the entire sheet of dough, gather the remaining dough, roll out again, and repeat the cutting process until all of the dough is used.

Using cookie cutters: Roll out the dough according to the directions for the cookie you are making. Dip the cutter into flour and then cut through the dough. Wiggle the cutter as you're cutting to be sure that it goes all the way through the dough. After cutting from the entire sheet of dough, gather the remaining dough, roll it out again, and repeat the cutting process until all of the dough is used.

Shortcut method: Follow the rolling instructions in the cookie recipe and leave the rolled-out dough on the parchment paper. Transfer the dough and the parchment paper to the baking sheet. Make the cuts with the cookie cutter or knife, leaving $1/2$ inch between cookies, and then, using both hands, carefully lift the edges of the unused dough and remove. The cookies will be perfectly spaced on the baking sheet. The paper can remain in place during baking.

Cutting complicated cookie shapes: When cutting holes or other shapes into a cookie, first cut the outer shape and transfer the cookie to the baking sheet. Then, using the appropriate tool (such as a straw for holes), cut out the interior shape. This will ensure that you don't break the shape. Also, when making cookies on a stick, it's best to press the popsicle stick or skewer into the dough after the cookies have been transferred to the baking sheet so that the stick doesn't fall out.

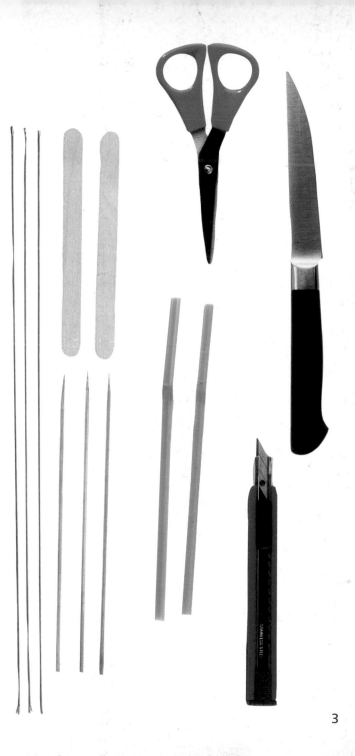

BUTTER COOKIES

Makes about 45 small or 25 large cookies

1 cup unsalted butter, cold

1 cup sugar

3 large eggs

1 teaspoon pure
    vanilla extract

3 1/2 cups all-purpose
    flour, sifted

1

Preheat the oven to 350°F. Place the butter and sugar in the bowl of a stand mixer or in a mixing bowl. With the dough hook or an electric mixer on high speed, cream the butter and sugar until light and creamy. Add the eggs 1 at a time, beating well on low speed after each addition. Add the vanilla and mix well on low speed. Add the flour 1 cup at a time, mixing well on low speed after each addition. (See steps 2–4 on page 5.)

GINGERBREAD COOKIES

Makes about 30 medium or 20 large cookies

3 cups all-purpose flour

1 teaspoon baking soda

1/2 cup unsalted butter, cold

1/2 cup packed brown sugar

1 large egg

1/2 cup corn syrup

2 teaspoons ground ginger

2 teaspoons ground cinnamon

1 teaspoon ground nutmeg

1

Preheat the oven to 350°F. Sift together the flour and baking soda into a bowl. Place the butter and sugar in the bowl of a stand mixer or in a mixing bowl. With the dough hook or an electric mixer on high speed, cream the butter and sugar until light and creamy. Add the egg and beat well on low speed. Add the corn syrup, ginger, cinnamon, and nutmeg and mix just until combined. Add the flour mixture 1 cup at a time, mixing well on low speed after each addition. (See steps 2–4 on page 5.)

CHOCOLATE COOKIES

Makes about 45 small or 25 large cookies

3 cups all-purpose flour
1/2 cup unsweetened cocoa powder
1 cup unsalted butter, cold
1 cup sugar
3 large eggs
1 teaspoon pure vanilla extract

1

Preheat the oven to 350°F. Sift together the flour and cocoa powder into a bowl. Place the butter and sugar in the bowl of a stand mixer or in a mixing bowl. With the dough hook or an electric mixer on high speed, cream the butter and sugar until light and creamy. Add the eggs 1 at a time, beating well on low speed after each addition. Add the vanilla and mix well. Add the flour mixture 1 cup at a time, mixing well on low speed after each addition.

2

Mix the dough just until a ball is formed, taking care not to overwork it; it should be rather stiff but not sticky. If the dough becomes too stiff, add water 1 teaspoon at a time.

3

Divide the dough into 2 balls. Wrap 1 ball with plastic wrap and set aside. Transfer the other ball onto a piece of parchment paper and flatten it out with your hands. Cover with another sheet of parchment paper. Using a rolling pin placed on top of the paper, roll out the dough to a thickness of 1/8 inch. Repeat with the other ball of dough.

4

Cut out your desired cookie shapes (see pages 2–3). Using a lightly floured metal spatula, transfer the cookies to an ungreased baking sheet. Allow 1/2 inch of space between the cookies. Place the baking sheet on the center rack in the oven. Bake for 6 to 8 minutes, until golden and crisped. Remove from the oven and let the cookies cool for 30 to 40 minutes on the baking sheet.

icing & decoration

the icing used for cookie decoration is sweet and hardens like candy when air-dried. Each batch of icing is enough to decorate one batch of cookies. The icing can be made with egg whites, or with meringue powder if you prefer not to use raw eggs. Meringue powder is available at specialty baking stores and through catalogs. There is no difference in quality between the two types. Prior to use, egg white icing can be stored in the refrigerator in an air-tight container for up to 3 days. Meringue powder icing can be stored at room temperature in an air-tight container for up to 2 weeks.

Cover the icing while working to prevent it from forming a crust, and remember to always use grease-free bowls and mixing utensils. To be certain that your utensils are grease free, wipe them with a paper towel dampened with white vinegar before using.

EGG WHITE ROYAL ICING

Makes 3 cups

3 large egg whites
1 tablespoon water
3 cups sifted confectioners' sugar

MERINGUE POWDER ROYAL ICING

Makes 3 cups

3 tablespoons meringue powder
7 tablespoons water
3 cups sifted confectioners' sugar

1

Place all three ingredients for either icing recipe in the bowl of a stand mixer or in a mixing bowl.

2

With the whisk attachment or an electric mixer, beat on low speed for about 10 minutes, until the mixture is the consistency of very thick cream. (You can also whisk the icing by hand, gradually adding the sugar to the meringue powder and water.) To test for the right consistency, scoop out a spoonful of icing and pour it back into the bowl. If it merges back into the mixture within 10 seconds, the consistency is correct.

3

Cover the icing with plastic wrap until ready to use.

icing consistency

There are three icing consistencies used for decorating, and which ones you'll need will depend on the type of decoration you're creating. Before decorating, count how many colors and consistencies you'll be using and divide the icing into separate bowls. Follow these directions for adjusting consistency.

Thin icing: Used to cover the cookie surface. It should resemble the consistency of very thick cream. Both of the icing recipes are designed to have thin consistency.

Medium icing: Used to draw faces and write letters. It should have the consistency of sour cream. For medium icing, decrease the amount of water by 1 tablespoon in either of the icing recipes.

Stiff icing: Used to pipe details that protrude from the surface, such as hair and swirls. It should resemble stiffly beaten egg whites. To make stiff icing from either of the recipes, add extra confectioners' sugar 1 teaspoon at a time until peaks form.

icing tools

There are a few specific tools you'll need for the decorations in this book.

Coupler: Used with a pastry bag, the coupler consists of two plastic parts that fit the bag from the inside and outside like a screw and bolt. The two parts secure the tip to the bag.

Decorating tips: Available in a variety of shapes and sizes, decorating tips are used with pastry bags to pipe icing onto the cookie. Round tips are used for outlines, letters, dots, and beads. Open star tips are used for making stars, flowers, and shells. Petal tips are used for making bows and ribbed stripes.

Paintbrushes: Good-quality sable brushes are used to paint and decorate with powders and gold dust. Small brushes (which are recommended) can be found at art supply stores.

Pastry bags: All of the cookies in this book require the use of pastry bags fitted with decorating tips for piping the icing. They are easy to use—even kids can manage them. You can buy dishwasher-safe, reusable polyester bags or disposable decorating bags at specialty baking stores or through mail-order catalogs.

icing colors & other decorations

Concentrated gel coloring is the best form of color to add to a basic white icing. You can also use liquid or powdered colorings, but the gel colorings are the easiest to use and produce the most vivid colors. Gel coloring for icing is available in specialty stores, at craft shops, or through mail-order catalogs specializing in baking products. There are more than thirty colors to choose from and you can mix them to create an endless variety. The colors are nontoxic and don't leave an aftertaste.

To add color to basic white icing, start with a fresh batch of icing (see page 7). Begin by dipping a toothpick into the color gel and then adding the color to the icing with the tip of the toothpick. Mix in the color with a spatula, adding color a little bit at a time until you achieve the desired shade. The colors—whether in gel or liquid form—are very concentrated, so start light and add with care. You can always add a dot of color to intensify the shade. Also take into consideration when coloring that tinted icing will darken 1 to 2 hours after mixing.

In addition to icing, a few other edible decorations are used for the cookies in this book:

Candies: Tiny treats like M&Ms and silver and gold dragées are adhered to the cookie with a little bit of icing

Colored sugar and sprinkles: These more common but wonderfully lively decorations add sparkle, texture, and color. They are sprinkled on top of the icing or atop a layer of egg white to help them stick.

Edible gold leaf: An elegant decoration used in fine pastry, edible gold leaf adds a gold shimmer to a cookie. It is applied with tweezers to a coating of egg white, which adheres it to the cookie.

Gold powder: Also known as "luster dust," gold powder is applied using a small paintbrush.

Pink petal dust: Also known as "luster dust," pink petal dust is applied using a small paintbrush.

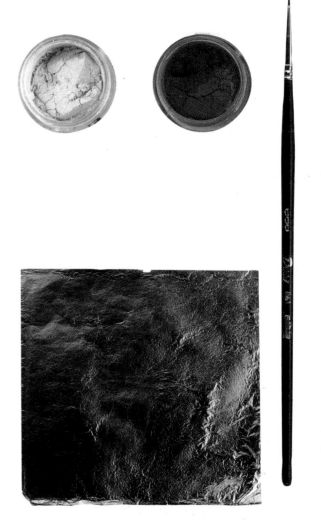

decorating techniques

Be sure to use a different pastry bag for each icing color so you don't have to stop and wash out the bag multiple times while making one design. The couplers allow you to switch out decorating tips, so you can apply one icing in many different ways without a lot of bags. If the icing hardens in the tip, insert a toothpick to unclog.

Filling the bag: Before filling the bag with icing you must attach the coupler and tip. Fit the plastic tip (larger piece) of the coupler on the inside lower edge of the bag. Insert the metal decorating tip through the coupler. Screw the round (smaller) part of the coupler onto the outside of the bag. Roll the edges of the bag down like a sleeve. Use a spatula to scoop in the icing, unrolling the bag as you go. Don't fill the bag more than three-quarters full; there should be plenty of bag left to twist off the filling. Tightly grip the bag near the top between your thumb and fingers. Twist, turn, and squeeze the bag. Hold your other hand close to the tip of the bag and use this hand to guide it.

Piping the icing: Piping the icing in the right direction and at the correct angle is very important. There are two angles to use: a 90-degree angle, straight and perpendicular to the surface, and a 45-degree angle, which is halfway between the perpendicular and horizontal. A right-handed person should work from left to right and a left-handed person from right to left. The icing flows by squeezing and applying pressure on the decorating bag. Practice first on a piece of parchment paper to learn how hard to squeeze and when to relax the grip on the bag. Pipe various decorations on the paper using different tips. The samples will harden and you can eat them as candy.

Outlining the cookie: Use a small round tip and thin icing. Holding the bag at a 45-degree angle, place the tip on the surface of the cookie, and squeeze the bag to start the flow of icing. Follow the outline of the cookie with the tip. To finish an outline, stop squeezing, press the tip into the surface of the cookie, and quickly lift it off. This will end the line without leaving a tail.

Covering the whole surface: Use a small round tip and thin icing. Holding the bag at a 45-degree angle, place the tip on the surface of the cookie and squeeze the bag to start the flow of icing. Let the icing flow continuously from the bag, working in zigzag (back and forth) motions until the surface is covered.

Writing letters: Use a small round tip and thin or medium icing. Holding the bag at a 45-degree angle, place the tip on the surface of the cookie and squeeze the bag to make the letters. For letters with straight edges, stop applying pressure and lift the tip from the surface at the end of the line to prevent tails. For round letters, apply continuous pressure and don't lift the tip until the letter is complete.

Dots: Use a small round tip and medium icing. Holding the bag at a 90-degree angle, keep the tip slightly above the surface of the cookie. Squeeze the bag to make the dot until it is the size you want. Stop pressure and pull away. Use a larger tip for big dots. You will have to occasionally clean the decorating tip with a dry paper towel.

Rosettes and hair: Use a star tip and stiff icing. Holding the bag at a 90-degree angle, keep the tip slightly above the surface of the cookie. Squeeze the bag until the rosette is the size you want. Stop pressure and pull the bag straight up. Clean the tip with a paper towel if necessary. Use a larger star tip for big rosettes. To achieve the look of curly hair, place the rosettes one beside the other.

Ribbons: Use a petal tip and medium or stiff icing. Hold the bag at a 45-degree angle with the ribbed side of the tip facing up. Place the tip on the surface of the cookie, squeeze the bag, and move your hand up and around to make the first loop of the ribbon. Keep squeezing the bag until the loop is the size you want. Stop pressure and pull away. Make the opposite loop the same way. From the meeting point of the loops, pipe the streams of the ribbon with the smooth side of the tip facing up. Squeeze the bag to make each tail until it is the length you want. Stop pressure and pull away.

cookie designs

getting ready to decorate

each set of instructions in this book describes a specific cookie design that appears on the same page, and gives the quantities of icing needed for a whole batch of that design. But don't let that stop you from getting creative: the best part of cookie decoration is the mixing and matching and experimenting with your own ideas and favorite colors. No matter what size your cookies, 3 cups of icing will always cover one batch of cookies. Be sure to always let the icing dry for at least 2 hours before serving.

PREPARATION

1 recipe cookie dough (pages 4–5)
1 recipe Royal Icing (page 7)
Gel food coloring

1. Roll out the cookie dough and cut out your desired shapes (see pages 2–3 for instructions). Bake the cookies according to the recipe directions and let them cool completely.

   Note: For designs with holes inside the cut-out cookie, use a straw to punch the holes after cutting out the larger shape but before baking. Popsicle sticks and skewers should also be pressed into dough before baking. It's best to do these things after you transfer the cookies to the baking sheet so that they don't lose their shape on the way there.

2. Divide the icing according to the consistency and amount of each color necessary for the design you wish to make. Tint each batch with the appropriate gel food coloring (see page 10 for instructions).

3. Fit the pastry bags with the decorating tips called for by the design and fill each one with one color of icing (see page 12 for instructions).

birthday

What a sweet and colorful way to say "Happy Birthday!"

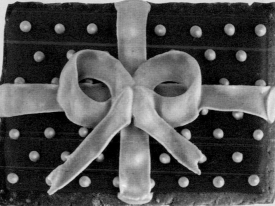

CLOWN

(pattern page 105)

1 batch Butter Cookies

3 cups Royal Icing, divided and tinted with gel food coloring to make:

    1 cup blue, thin consistency

    1 cup white, thin consistency

    ¼ cup pink, thin consistency

    ¼ cup yellow, thin consistency

    ¼ cup red, thin consistency

    ¼ cup peach, thin consistency

6 pastry bags and couplers

Decorating tips: round #2, #3, and #4; open star #20

1. Using a round tip #3, pipe a blue outline around the clown hat.

2. Using a round tip #4, pipe blue icing to cover the surface of the hat up to the outline.

3. Using a round tip #4, pipe white icing to cover the round part of the cookie for the face. Let dry for 30 minutes.

4. Using a round tip #2, pipe pink icing for the dots on the hat.

5. Using a round tip #2, pipe white icing in a thick line for the mouth.

6. Using a round tip #2, pipe blue icing for the eyes.

7. Using a round tip #2, pipe a yellow zigzag line at the bottom of the hat.

8. Using a round tip #4, pipe red icing in a thin line for the smile and a big dot for the nose.

9. Using an open star tip #20, pipe peach icing for the ears.

PRESENT

(pattern page 105)

1 batch Butter Cookies

3 cups Royal Icing, divided and tinted with gel food coloring to make:

   1½ cups pink, thin consistency

   ½ cup purple, thin consistency

   1 cup yellow, medium consistency

3 pastry bags and couplers

Decorating tips: round #2 and #4; petal #101

1. Using a round tip #4, pipe pink icing to cover the cookie surface. Let dry for 30 minutes.

2. Using a round tip #2, pipe purple icing for decorations such as polka dots or squiggles. Let dry for 30 minutes.

3. Using a petal tip #101, pipe yellow icing for the bow.

BANNER

(pattern page 106)

1 batch Butter Cookies

3 cups Royal Icing, divided and tinted with gel food coloring to make:

    1½ cups pink, thin consistency

    1 cup light blue, medium consistency

    1½ cup yellow, thin consistency

3 pastry bags and couplers

Decorating tips: round #2, #3, and #4

Plastic straw

Narrow yellow silk ribbons

1. After cutting out the cookie shapes but before baking, use the straw to punch a small hole through each end of the cookie. Bake and cool as instructed.

2. Using a round tip #3, pipe a pink outline around each cookie.

3. Using a round tip #4, pipe pink icing to cover the cookie surface up to the outline. Let dry for 30 minutes.

4. Using a round tip #2, pipe light blue icing to write "Happy Birthday" on the cookie.

5. Using a round tip #2, pipe yellow icing for dots along the upper and bottom edges.

6. Let the cookies dry for at least 2 hours, then thread a yellow silk ribbon through the holes before serving.

BALLOON

(pattern page 105)

1 batch Butter Cookies

3 cups Royal Icing, divided and
    tinted with gel food coloring
    to make:

    2$\frac{1}{2}$ cups red, thin consistency

    $\frac{1}{2}$ cup yellow, thin
      consistency

2 pastry bags and couplers

Decorating tips: round #2, #3,
    and #4

1. Using a round tip #3, pipe a red outline around the cookie.

2. Using a round tip #4, pipe red icing to cover the cookie surface up to the outline. Let dry for 30 minutes.

3. Using a round tip #3, pipe a red outline on top of the first outline to create a bold border.

4. Using a round tip #3, pipe red icing for 2 vertical lines near the base of the balloon to represent the pleats. Let dry for 30 minutes.

5. Using a round tip #2, pipe yellow icing in a horizontal line to represent the string at the base of the balloon.

CUPCAKE

(pattern page 105)

1 batch Butter Cookies

3 cups Royal Icing, divided and tinted with gel
   food coloring to make:
     1¾ cups white, thin consistency
     1¼ cups light blue, thin consistency

2 pastry bags and couplers

Decorating tips: round #3 and #4; open star #20

Red M&M candies

Green-colored sprinkles

1

Using a round tip #3, pipe white icing in a
trapezoid shape to outline the lower portion of
the cookie.

2

Using a round tip #4, pipe white icing to cover
the cookie surface within the outline. Let dry
for 30 minutes.

3

Using a round tip #3, pipe white icing on top
of the first outline to create a bold border and
then in three vertical lines on the bottom of the
cookie. Let dry for 10 minutes.

4

Using an open star tip #20, pipe blue icing to
create the frosting.

5

Place a red M&M candy on top of the frosting,
using a little of the blue icing to glue the candy
down.

6

Scatter green sprinkles on the blue frosting.

wedding

These elegant and sweet cookies make a great favor for your wedding guests.

WEDDING CAKE

(pattern page 106)

1 batch Butter Cookies

3 cups Royal Icing, divided and tinted with gel food coloring to make:

    2¼ cups white, thin consistency

    5 tablespoons yellow, thin consistency

    5 tablespoons light pink, thin consistency

    2 tablespoons purple, thin consistency

4 pastry bags and couplers

Decorating tips: round #2 and #3

1. Using a round tip #3, pipe white icing to cover the surface of the cookie, leaving the top tier uncovered. Let dry for 30 minutes.

2. Using a round tip #2, pipe a white icing outline on top of the first layer to create a bold border.

3. Using a round tip #2, pipe white icing for decorations such as polka dots, squiggles, hearts, and waves.

4. Using a round tip #2, pipe yellow icing for beads on the bottom tier and a scalloped line on the second tier.

5. Using a round tip #3, pipe light pink icing for a heart on the top tier.

6. Using a round tip #2, pipe purple icing for beads along the scalloped line.

BRIDAL DRESS

(pattern page 106)

1 batch Butter Cookies

3 cups Royal Icing, divided and
  tinted with gel food coloring
  to make:

  2¹/₂ cups white, thin
    consistency

  ¹/₂ cup light pink, thin
    consistency

2 pastry bags and couplers

Decorating tips: round #2
  and #4

1. Using a round tip #4, pipe white icing to cover the surface of
   the cookie. Let dry for 30 minutes.

2. Using a round tip #2, pipe a light pink outline on top of the
   first layer to create a bold border.

3. Using a round tip #2, pipe light pink icing for the waistline,
   pleat lines, dots, and the heart on the corset.

FLOWER BOUQUET

(patterns page 107)

2 batches Butter Cookies

6 cups Royal Icing, divided and tinted with gel food coloring to make:

Big Flower

1/2 cup pink, thin consistency

1 1/2 cups yellow, thin consistency

1 cup orange, thin consistency

Small Flower

1 cup red, thin consistency

1/2 cup yellow, thin consistency

Leaf

1 1/2 cups green, thin consistency

5 pastry bags and couplers

Decorating tips: round #3

Metal skewers

Narrow pink silk ribbons

1. After cutting out the cookie shapes but before baking, press a metal skewer into the bottom edge of each flower and leaf cutout to form a stem. Bake and cool as instructed, then place the cookies on the work surface with the stick side facing up.

2. For the Big Flower, using a round tip #3, pipe a pink outline around the petals of the flower. This will help glue the skewer to the cookie. Let dry for 30 minutes.

3. Using a round tip #3, pipe yellow icing to cover the petals within the pink outline. Let dry for 30 minutes.

4. Using a round tip #3, pipe orange icing to cover the center of the flower.

5. For the Small Flower, using a round tip #3, pipe red icing to cover the petals of the flower. Let dry for 30 minutes.

6. Using a round tip #3, pipe yellow icing to cover the center of the flower.

7. For the Leaf, using a round tip #3, pipe a green outline around the cookie.

8. Using a round tip #3, pipe green icing to cover the surface of the cookie up to the outline. Let dry for 30 minutes.

9. Using a round tip #3, pipe a green outline on top of the first layer to create a bold border.

10. Using a round tip #3, pipe a green squiggly line to represent the vein of the leaf.

11. Let the cookies dry for at least 2 hours, then tie the metal skewers together with a pink silk ribbon to form the bouquet before serving.

HEART OF GOLD

(pattern page 108)

1 batch Butter Cookies

3 cups white Royal Icing, thin consistency

1 decorating bag and coupler

Decorating tips: round #2, #3, and #4

Paintbrush

1 egg white

Tweezers

Edible gold leaf

1

Using a round tip #3, pipe a white outline, leaving a $1/8$-inch edge all around.

2

Using a round tip #4, pipe white icing to cover the surface of the cookie up to the outline. Let dry for 12 hours.

3

Using a paintbrush dipped in egg white, dot the surface of the cookie in several places.

5

Using a round tip #3, pipe a white outline on top of the first layer to create a bold border.

4

Using the tweezers, gently place pieces of the gold leaf on the egg white. Press gently with a dry brush to set the gold leaf into the surface. (The egg white helps the gold leaf stick.)

6

Using a round tip #2, pipe white icing for dots all around the border.

baby shower

Such cute cookies to celebrate the birth of a baby. Give them to guests at a baby shower or use them as charming and unique birth announcements.

BABY BOTTLE

(pattern page 108)

1 batch Butter Cookies

3 cups Royal Icing, divided and tinted with gel food coloring to make:

2 cups white, thin consistency

1/2 cup pink, thin consistency

1/4 cup orange, thin consistency

1/4 cup purple, thin consistency

4 pastry bags and couplers

Decorating tips: round #2, #3, and #4

1. Using a round tip #3, pipe a white outline in a rectangle around the body of the bottle.

2. Using a round tip #4, pipe white icing to cover the surface of the cookie within the rectangle. Let dry for 30 minutes.

3. Using a round tip #3, pipe a pink outline on top of the first outline to create a bold border.

4. Using a round tip #3, pipe orange icing to cover the surface of the nipple. Let dry for 30 minutes.

5. Using a round tip #2, pipe pink icing in the shape of a rectangle to form the collar between the nipple and the bottle. Let dry for 30 minutes.

6. Using a round tip #3, pipe pink icing for the vertical lines on the collar and the horizontal lines on the bottle.

7. Using a round tip #2, pipe purple icing to decorate the bottle with dots and hearts.

BODYSUIT

(pattern page 109)

1 batch Butter Cookies

3 cups Royal Icing, divided and tinted with gel food coloring to make:

    2 cups plus 6 tablepsoons light blue, thin consistency

    1/2 cup dark blue, thin consistency

    2 tablespoons green, thin consistency

3 pastry bags and couplers

Decorating tips: round #2 and #4

1. Using a round tip #2, pipe a light blue outline to form the shape of a bodysuit.

2. Using a round tip #4, pipe light blue icing to cover the surface of the cookie within the outline. Let dry for 30 minutes.

3. Using a round tip #2, pipe a light blue outline on top of the first layer to create a bold border. Let dry for 10 minutes.

4. Using a round tip #2, pipe dark blue icing for the scallops at the leg holes.

5. Using a round tip #2, pipe dark blue icing along the neck and for the spiral in the center.

6. Using a round tip #2, pipe green dots to represent the snaps along the bottom.

ALPHABET BLOCKS

(pattern page 109)

1 batch Butter Cookies

3 cups Royal Icing, divided and tinted with gel food coloring to make:

   3/4 cup lavender, thin consistency

   3/4 cup light blue, thin consistency

   3/4 cup light yellow, thin consistency

   1/4 cup white, medium consistency

   1/4 cup pink, medium consistency

   1/4 cup purple, medium consistency

6 pastry bags and couplers

Decorating tips: round #2 and #3

1. Using a round tip #3, pipe lavender icing to outline the top cube.

2. Using a round tip #3, pipe lavender icing to cover the surface of the top cube up to the outline. Let dry for 10 minutes.

3. Using a round tip #3, pipe light blue icing to outline the right cube.

4. Using a round tip #3, pipe light blue icing to cover the surface of the right cube up to the outline. Let dry for 10 minutes.

5. Using a round tip #3, pipe light yellow icing to outline the left cube.

6. Using a round tip #3, pipe light yellow icing to cover the surface of the left cube up to the outline. Let dry for 30 minutes.

7. Using a round tip #2, pipe white icing for the letter on the lavender cube. For bolder letters, draw several lines next to each other.

8. Using a round tip #2, pipe pink icing for the letter on the light blue cube.

9. Using a round tip #2, pipe purple icing for the letter on the yellow cube.

BABY BOY/BABY GIRL

(pattern page 110)

1 batch Butter Cookies

3 cups Royal Icing, divided and tinted with gel food coloring to make:

　2 cups off-white, thin consistency

　$^1/_2$ cup light blue, stiff consistency

　$^1/_4$ cup red, thin consistency

　$^1/_4$ cup orange, thin consistency

4 pastry bags and couplers

Decorating tips: round #2 and #4; petal #101

Small paintbrush

Pink petal dust

Orange gel food coloring

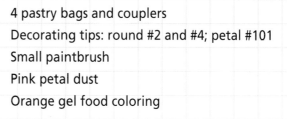

1

Using a round tip #4, pipe an off-white outline around the cookie, leaving a $^1/_8$-inch edge all around.

2

Using a round tip #4, pipe off-white icing to cover the surface up to the outline. Let dry for 30 minutes.

3

Using a round tip #2, pipe off-white dots for the nose and ears.

4

Using a petal tip #101, pipe light blue icing for the hair at the top of the cookie and for the bow on the bottom.

5

Using a round tip #2, pipe light blue icing dots for the eyes.

6

Using a round tip #2, pipe red icing for the mouth.

7

Using a small paintbrush, paint pink petal dust in small circles on the cheeks.

8

Dip the brush directly into the orange gel coloring and draw a line above each eye for the eyebrows.

9

Using a round tip #2, pipe orange icing in a squiggly line for the bangs.

be my valentine

These colorful cookies are just a few beautiful ways to say "I love you" to your Valentine—or anyone else.

HEART ON A STICK

(pattern page 110)

1 batch Butter Cookies

3 cups Royal Icing, divided and tinted with gel food coloring to make:

  2 cups lavender, thin consistency

  1 cup pink, thin consistency

2 pastry bags and couplers

Decorating tips: round #2 and #4

Wooden skewers

1. After cutting out the cookie shapes but before baking, press a wooden skewer into the bottom edge of each heart. Bake and cool as instructed, then place the cookies on the work surface with the skewer side facing up.

2. Using a round tip #4, pipe lavender icing to cover the surface of the cookie, leaving a $1/8$-inch edge all around. Let dry for 30 minutes.

3. Using a round tip #2, pipe pink decorations onto the surface of the cookie, such as polka dots and hearts.

4. Using a round tip #2, pipe pink decorations onto the border of the cookie, such as lines or lace.

COLORFUL HEARTS

(pattern page 108)

1 batch Butter Cookies

3 cups Royal Icing, divided and tinted with gel food coloring to make:

    2 cups red, thin consistency

    1/2 cup yellow, thin consistency

    1/2 cup orange, thin consistency

3 pastry bags and couplers

Decorating tips: round #2 and #4

1. Using a round tip #2, pipe a red outline around each cookie.

2. Using a round tip #4, pipe red icing to cover the surface of the cookie up to the outline. Let dry for 30 minutes.

3. Using a round tip #2, pipe yellow lines onto the cookie.

4. Using a round tip #2, pipe an orange outline around the cookie to create a bold border.

VALENTINE'S DAY CARD

(pattern page 105)

1 batch Butter Cookies

3 cups Royal Icing, divided and tinted with gel food coloring to make:

    2 cups pink, thin consistency

    1/2 cup lavender, thin consistency

    1/2 cup red, thin consistency

3 pastry bags and couplers

Decorating tips: round #2 and #4

1. Using a round tip #4, pipe pink icing to cover the cookie surface, leaving a 1/4-inch edge at the top and bottom. Let dry for 30 minutes.

2. Using a round tip #2, pipe a lavender outline on top of the pink icing to create a bold border. Let dry for 10 minutes.

3. Using a round tip #2, pipe lavender icing to write your special message of love.

4. Using a round tip #2, pipe lavender icing for the dots all along the edges.

5. Using a round tip #2, pipe red icing to decorate the top and bottom edges of the cookie with hearts.

easter

Fill your Easter basket with lots of colorful cookies. The Easter bunny will love them—and so will the kids!

EASTER EGG

(pattern page 110)

1 batch Butter Cookies

3 cups Royal Icing, divided and tinted with gel food coloring to make:

    2 cups light blue, thin consistency

    1 cup pink, thin consistency

2 pastry bags and couplers

Decorating tips: round #3 and #4

1. Using a round tip #3, pipe a light blue outline around the cookie.

2. Using a round tip #4, pipe light blue icing to cover the surface of the cookie up to the outline. Do not let the icing dry.

3. Using a round tip #3, immediately pipe pink icing for the dots. (Working quickly without letting the icing dry will allow the dots to sink into the surface of the first color.)

EASTER BUNNY

(pattern page 110)

1 batch Butter Cookies

3 cups Royal Icing, divided and tinted with gel
  food coloring to make:

  $2^{1}/_{4}$ cups purple, thin consistency

  $^{1}/_{2}$ cup light blue, medium consistency

  $^{1}/_{4}$ cup red, thin consistency

3 pastry bags and couplers

Decorating tips: round #2, #3, and #4; petal #101

Small paintbrush

1 egg white

Purple-colored sugar

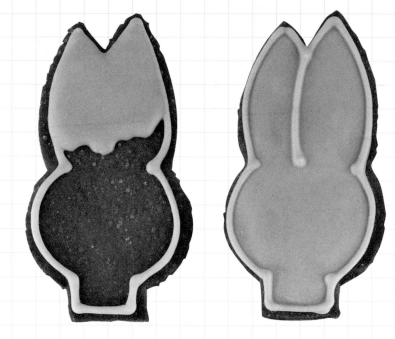

1

Using a round tip #3, pipe a purple outline
around the cookie.

2

Using a round tip #4, pipe purple icing to cover
the surface of the cookie up to the outline. Let
dry for 30 minutes.

3

Using a round tip #3, pipe a purple outline on
top of the dry outline to create a bold border.

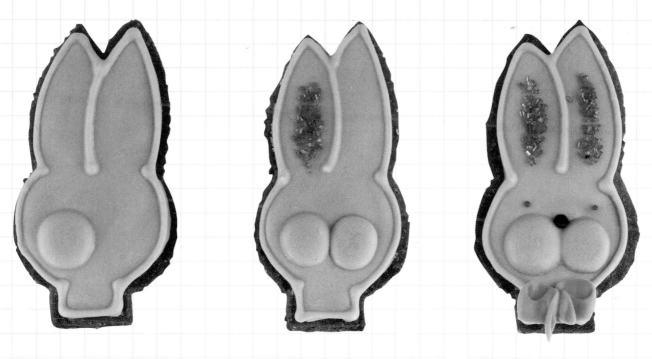

4

Using a round tip #3, pipe purple icing in two large circles next to each other in the middle of the face. Let dry for 30 minutes.

5

Using a small paintbrush, brush egg white onto the middle of each ear.

6

Sprinkle the colored sugar over the egg white. The egg white will glue the sugar to the surface.

7

Using a petal tip #101, pipe light blue icing for the bow at the bottom of the cookie.

8

Using a round tip #2, pipe light blue icing dots for the eyes.

9

Using a round tip #2, pipe a red icing dot between the two purple circles to represent the nose.

july 4th

Celebrate Independence Day in style with an array of patriotic cookies.

FIRECRACKER

(pattern page 111)

1 batch Butter Cookies

3 cups Royal Icing, divided and tinted with gel food coloring to make:

  1 cup red, thin consistency

  1/4 cup blue, thin consistency

  1 cup white, thin consistency

  1/4 cup black, thin consistency

  1/2 cup yellow, thin consistency

5 pastry bags and couplers

Decorating tips: round #2, #3, and #4

Toothpicks

1. Using a round tip #4, pipe red icing to cover the rectangular surface of the cookie (the body of the firecracker). Do not let the icing dry.

2. Using a round tip #3, immediately pipe blue dots all over the surface of the rectangle. Do not let the icing dry.

3. Using a toothpick, immediately drag the dots in wavy motions into the red icing. Let dry for 30 minutes.

4. Using a round tip #4, pipe white icing to cover the surface of the pointy top of the cookie (the explosion). Let dry for 30 minutes.

5. Using a round tip #3, pipe a black flame in the center of the white surface.

6. Using a round tip #2, pipe yellow icing in squiggly lines on top of the white surface.

AMERICAN FLAG

(pattern page 111)

1 batch Butter Cookies

3 cups Royal Icing, divided and tinted with gel food coloring to make:

  2 cups white, thin consistency

  ½ cup blue, thin consistency

  ½ cup red, medium consistency

3 pastry bags and couplers

Decorating tips: round #2, #3, and #4

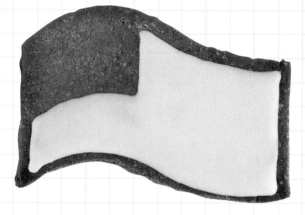

1

Using a round tip #3, pipe a white outline around the striped part of the flag.

2

Using a round tip #4, pipe white icing to cover the surface of the cookie up to the outline. Let dry for 30 minutes.

3

Using a round tip #3, pipe a blue rectangular outline in the upper left corner.

4

Using a round tip #3, pipe blue icing to fill the rectangle. Let dry for 30 minutes.

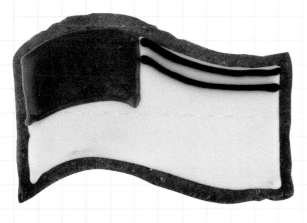

5

Using a round tip #2, pipe red icing in wavy stripes on the white part of the cookie.

6

Using a round tip #2, pipe white icing dots for the stars on the blue rectangle.

halloween

Put some scary cookies in those trick-or-treat bags and yours will be the most popular house in the neighborhood!

JACK O'LANTERN

(pattern page 112)

1 batch Butter Cookies

3 cups Royal Icing, divided and tinted with gel food coloring to make:

   2 cups orange, thin consistency

   $7/8$ cup black, thin consistency

   2 tablespoons green, medium consistency

3 pastry bags and couplers

Decorating tips: round #2 and #4

1. Using a round tip #4, pipe orange icing to cover the cookie surface to the edge. Let dry for 30 minutes.

2. Using a round tip #2, pipe black icing for the eyes and mouth. Let dry for 30 minutes.

3. Using a round tip #2, pipe a black outline around the eyes and mouth to create a bold border.

4. Using a round tip #2, pipe orange icing around the edge of the jack o'lantern to create a bold border and to make the curving lines on the face.

5. Using a round tip #2, pipe green icing for the stem.

SPIDER

(pattern page 112)

1 batch Butter Cookies

3 cups Royal Icing, divided and tinted with gel food coloring to make:

    2 cups black, thin consistency

    2 tablespoons white, thin consistency

    3 tablespoons red, thin consistency

    3 tablespoons blue, thin consistency

    $1/2$ cup black, stiff consistency

5 pastry bags and couplers

Decorating tips: round #2, #3, and #4

1

Using a round tip #4, pipe thin black icing to form a circular outline in the middle of the cookie.

2

Using a round tip #4, pipe thin black icing to cover the inside of the circle.

3

Using a round tip #3, pipe thin black icing into 6 lines with sharp angles going out from the circle on both sides to represent the legs of the spider. Let dry for 30 minutes.

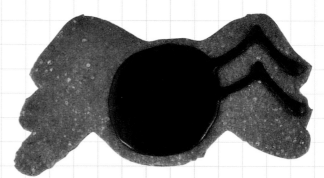

4

Using a round tip #2, pipe white dots for the eyes on the black circle.

5

Using a round tip #2, pipe red icing on the black circle for the mouth.

6

Using a round tip #2, pipe a blue dot on the black circle for the nose and small blue dots on the eyes.

7

Using a round tip #2, pipe stiff black icing to make pointy dots all over the surface of the black circle. To make pointy dots, pipe the dots and then lift the bag up so that the icing breaks from the tip.

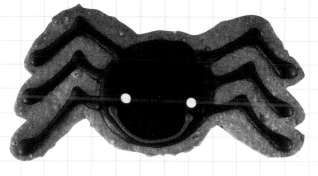

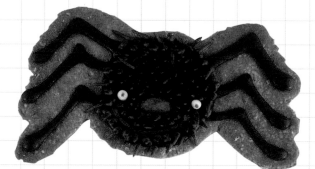

GHOST

(pattern page 112)

1 batch Butter Cookies

3 cups Royal Icing, divided and tinted with gel food coloring to make:

   2 1/2 cups white, thin consistency

   1/4 cup black, thin consistency

   1/4 cup red, thin consistency

3 pastry bags and couplers

Decorating tips: round #2, #3, and #4

1. Using a round tip #3, pipe a white outline around the cookie.

2. Using a round tip #4, pipe white icing to cover the surface of the cookie up to the outline. Let dry for 10 minutes.

3. Using a round tip #3, pipe a white outline on top of the dry outline to create a bold border. Let dry for 2 hours.

4. Using a round tip #3, pipe big black dots for the eyes.

5. Using a round tip #2, pipe a big red dot for a mouth.

6. Using a round tip #2, pipe white dots onto the black eyes.

thanksgiving

Give thanks and count your blessings with these symbolic cookies.

TURKEY

(pattern page 113)

1 batch Butter Cookies

3 cups Royal Icing, divided and tinted with gel food coloring to make:

    1 cup orange, thin consistency

    1 cup plus 3 tablespoons red, thin consistency

    3/4 cup brown, thin consistency

    1 tablespoon black, thin consistency

4 pastry bags and couplers

Decorating tips: round #2 and #4

Toothpicks

1. Using a round tip #4, pipe an orange outline around the top portion of the turkey.

2. Using a round tip #4, pipe orange icing to cover the area inside the outline. Do not let the icing dry.

3. Using a round tip #4, pipe a red outline around the lower left portion of the turkey.

4. Using a round tip #4, pipe red icing to fill the area inside the outline. Do not let the icing dry.

5. Using a toothpick, immediately drag the orange icing down into the red icing to achieve a feathery effect.

6. Using a round tip #4, pipe an orange outline on top of the first layer on the top portion of the turkey to create a bold border.

7. Using a round tip #4, pipe a brown outline around the right side of the turkey.

8. Using a round tip #4, pipe brown icing to cover the area inside the outline. Do not let the icing dry.

9. Using a toothpick, immediately drag the red icing into the brown icing to achieve a feathery effect. Let dry for 30 minutes.

10. Using a round tip #2, pipe a black icing dot for the eye.

11. Using a round tip #2, pipe red icing for the beak, wattle, and dots on the feathers.

CORN

(pattern page 113)

1 batch Butter Cookies

3 cups Royal Icing, divided and tinted with gel food coloring to make:

    2½ cups yellow, thin consistency

    ½ cup green, thin consistency

2 pastry bags and couplers

Decorating tips: round #3 and #4

1. Using a round tip #3, pipe a yellow outline around the corn cob.

2. Using a round tip #4, pipe yellow icing to cover the surface of the cookie within the outline. Let dry for 30 minutes.

3. Using a round tip #3, pipe green icing to cover the surface of the leaf. Let dry for 30 minutes.

4. Using a round tip #3, pipe evenly spaced large yellow dots on top of the yellow icing.

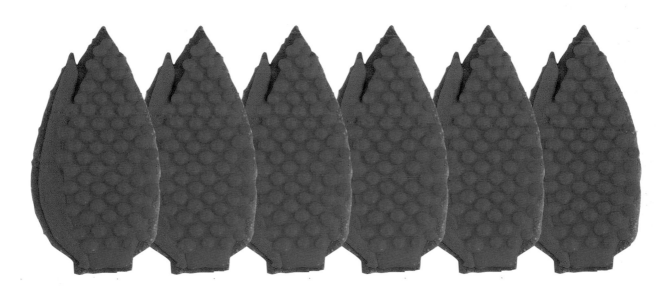

MAPLE LEAF

(pattern page 113)

1 batch Butter Cookies

3 cups Royal Icing, divided and tinted with gel food coloring to make:

    1 cup dark green, thin consistency

    1 cup light green, thin consistency

    1 cup yellow-green, thin consistency

3 pastry bags and couplers

Decorating tips: round #4

Toothpicks

2

Using a round tip #4, pipe light green icing in a thick line next to the dark green outline. Do not let the icing dry.

3

Using a toothpick, immediately drag the light green icing into the dark green to weave them into each other.

1

Using a round tip #4, pipe a dark green outline around half of the cookie.

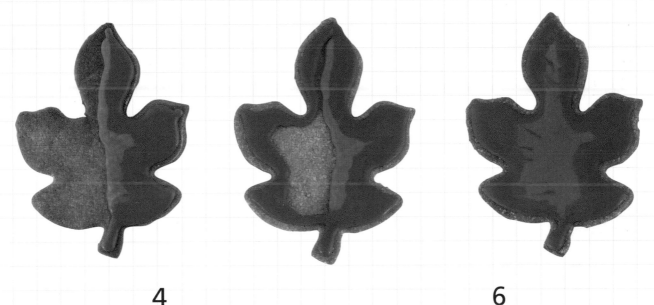

4

Using a round tip #4, pipe yellow-green icing in a thick line next to the light green icing. Do not let the icing dry.

5

Using a toothpick, immediately drag the yellow-green icing into the light green icing to weave them into each other.

6

Repeat the process on the other half of the cookie.

christmas

Add to the holiday cheer with these special Christmas cookies. Serve them to guests with warm milk or eggnog, or box them and send as homemade goodies to family and friends.

CHRISTMAS ORNAMENTS

(patterns page 114)

1 batch Butter Cookies

3 cups Royal Icing, divided and tinted with gel food coloring to make:

2½ cups red, thin consistency

¼ cup yellow, thin consistency

¼ cup green, thin consistency

3 pastry bags and couplers

Decorating tips: round #2 and #4

Small round cookie cutter

Narrow gold silk ribbons

1. After cutting out the cookie shapes but before baking, use the cookie cutter to make the large hole in the center of the cookie. Bake and cool as instructed.

2. Using a round tip #2, pipe a red outline around the inner and outer edges of the cookie.

3. Using a round tip #4, pipe red icing to cover the surface of the cookie up to the outline. Let dry for 30 minutes.

4. Using a round tip #2, pipe yellow dots around the outer edge. Let dry for 2 hours.

5. Using a round tip #2, pipe green icing for hearts to decorate the surface of the cookie.

6. Let the cookies dry for at least 12 hours.

7. Tie a gold ribbon through the hole in each cookie before serving.

SNOWMAN

(pattern page 115)

1 batch Butter Cookies

3 cups Royal Icing, divided and tinted with gel food coloring to make:

    2 cups white, thin consistency

    1/2 cup red, thin consistency

    2 tablespoons blue, thin consistency

    2 tablespoons orange, thin consistency

    1/4 green, thin consistency

5 pastry bags and couplers

Decorating tips: round #2 and #4

1. Using a round tip #2, pipe a white outline around each cookie.

2. Using a round tip #4, pipe white icing to cover the surface of the cookie up to the outline. Let dry for 30 minutes.

3. Using a round tip #2, pipe a white outline on top of the first layer to form a bold border.

4. Using a round tip #2, pipe red icing for the mouth.

5. Using a round tip #2, pipe blue dots for the eyes.

6. Using a round tip #2, pipe an orange dot for the nose.

7. Using a round tip #2, pipe red icing for the scarf. Let dry for 30 minutes.

8. Using a round tip #2, pipe green icing in parallel lines to stripe the scarf.

SANTA CLAUS

(pattern page 115)

1 batch Butter Cookies

3 cups Royal Icing, divided and tinted with gel food coloring to make:

    1/2 cup off-white, thin consistency

    1/2 cup plus 2 tablespoons red, thin consistency

    2 tablespoons blue, thin consistency

    1 3/4 cups white, stiff consistency

4 pastry bags and couplers

Decorating tips: round #2, #3, #4, and #6

1. Using a round tip #3, pipe off-white icing to cover the face.

2. Using a round tip #4, pipe red icing to cover the hat. Let dry for 30 minutes.

3. Using a round tip #2, pipe red icing for the mouth.

4. Using a round tip #2, pipe blue dots for the eyes.

5. Using a round tip #2, pipe a big off-white dot for the nose. Let dry for 30 minutes.

6. Using a round tip #6, pipe white icing for the hair, beard, and tip of the hat.

CHRISTMAS TREE

(pattern page 115)

1 batch Butter Cookies

3 cups Royal Icing, divided and tinted with gel food coloring to make:

    2¹/₂ cups green, thin consistency

    ¹/₂ cup yellow, thin consistency

2 decorating bags and couplers

Decorating tips: round #3 and #4

Tweezers

Gold dragée candies

1. Using a round tip #3, pipe a green outline around the cookie.

2. Using a round tip #4, pipe green icing to cover the surface of the cookie up to the outline. Let dry for 30 minutes.

3. Using a round tip #3, pipe a green outline on top of the first layer to create a bold border.

4. Using a round tip #3, pipe yellow icing to cover the star.

5. Using a round tip #3, pipe green icing in thin lines for the garlands and at the top of the tree. Do not let the icing dry.

6. Using tweezers, immediately place the yellow star and the gold dragée candies on the wet icing. The icing will glue them to the cookie.

ANGEL

(pattern page 116)

1 batch Butter Cookies

3 cups Royal Icing, divided and tinted with gel food coloring to make:

  1 cup purple, thin consistency

  ¼ cup off-white, thin consistency

  1 cup white, thin consistency

  2 tablespoons blue, thin consistency

  2 tablespoons red, thin consistency

  ¼ cup orange, stiff consistency

  ¼ cup yellow, thin consistency

7 pastry bags and couplers

Decorating tips: round #2, #3, and #4; open star #17

1. Using a round tip #2, pipe a purple outline around the dress.

2. Using a round tip #4, pipe purple icing to cover the surface of the dress up to the outline.

3. Using a round tip #3, pipe off-white icing to cover the face.

4. Using a round tip #4, pipe a white outline around the wings.

5. Using a round tip #4, pipe white icing to cover the wings up to the border. Let dry for 30 minutes.

6. Using a round tip #2, pipe a white outline on top of the first layer on the wings to form a bold border.

7. Using a round tip #2, pipe an off-white dot for the nose.

8. Using a round tip #2, pipe blue dots for the eyes.

9. Using a round tip #2, pipe red icing for the mouth.

10. Using an open star tip #17, pipe orange icing around the face to create the hair.

11. Using a round tip #2, pipe yellow icing to decorate the dress with dots and hearts.

STAR

(pattern page 116)

1 batch Butter Cookies

3 cups Royal Icing, tinted with blue gel food coloring, thin consistency

1 pastry bag and coupler

Decorating tips: round #3 and #4

Small paintbrush

Gold powder

Tweezers

Silver dragée candies

1

Using a round tip #3, pipe a blue outline around the cookie.

2

Using a round tip #4, pipe blue icing to cover the surface of the cookie up to the outline. Let dry for 30 minutes.

3

Using a round tip #3, pipe a blue outline on top of the first layer to create a bold border. Do not let the icing dry.

4

Using a small paintbrush, paint gold powder in the shape of little stars all over the surface.

5

Using tweezers, immediately place silver dragée candies on the wet icing at the points of the star.

hanukkah

Light up the Hanukkah holiday with a dreidel, menorah, and Hanukkah candles. Delight family and friends with these delicious symbols of tradition.

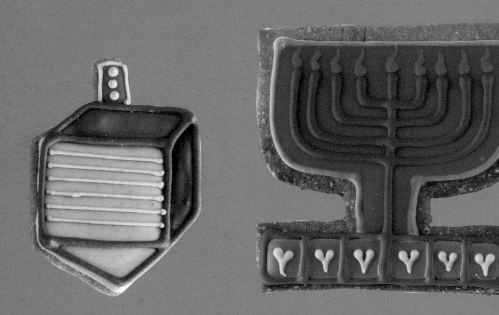

MENORAH

(pattern page 117)

1 batch Butter Cookies

3 cups Royal Icing, divided and tinted with gel food coloring to make:

    1 cup light green, thin consistency

    3/4 cup light blue, thin consistency

    3/4 cup orange, thin consistency

    1/4 cup yellow, thin consistency

    1/4 cup purple, thin consistency

5 pastry bags and couplers

Decorating tips: round #2, #3, and #4

1. Using a round tip #3, pipe a light green outline around the top part of the cookie (not the base).

2. Using a round tip #4, pipe light green icing to cover the surface of the top part of the cookie up to the outline (do not cover the base). Let dry for 30 minutes.

3. Using a round tip #4, pipe light blue icing to cover the surface of the base. Let dry for 30 minutes.

4. Using a round tip #2, pipe a light blue outline on top of the dry green icing on the top part of the cookie to create a bold border.

5. Using a round tip #2, pipe an orange outline and 5 vertical lines on top of the dry blue icing on the base.

6. Using a round tip #2, pipe orange icing to represent the branches and stem of the menorah. Let dry for 30 minutes.

7. Using a round tip #2, pipe yellow icing at the top of the branches to represent flames.

8. Using a round tip #2, pipe purple icing to create the hearts on the base.

HANUKKAH CANDLE

(pattern page 117)

1 batch Butter Cookies

3 cups Royal Icing, divided and tinted with gel food
coloring to make:

2 cups green, thin consistency

$\frac{1}{3}$ cup yellow, thin consistency

$\frac{1}{3}$ cup orange, thin consistency

$\frac{1}{3}$ cup blue, thin consistency

4 pastry bags and couplers

Decorating tips: round #2, #3, and #4

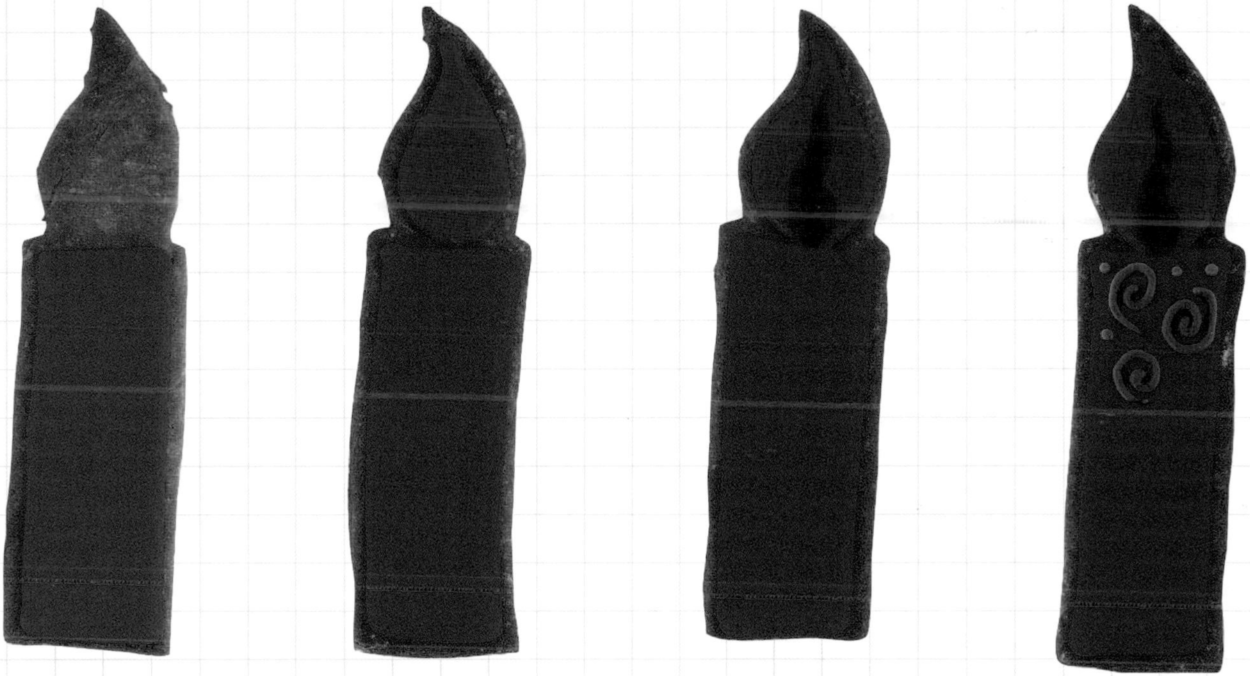

1

Using a round tip #4, pipe green icing to cover the rectangular surface of the cookie. Let dry for 30 minutes.

2

Using a round tip #3, pipe yellow icing to cover the surface of the flame. Do not let the icing dry.

3

Using a round tip #2, immediately pipe orange icing on top of the yellow flame in the shape of a squiggle.

4

Using a round tip #2, pipe blue icing to decorate the candle with dots and spirals.

DREIDEL

(pattern page 117)

1 batch Butter Cookies

3 cups Royal Icing, divided and tinted with gel food coloring to make:

    1 cup red, thin consistency

    1 cup yellow, thin consistency

    1/2 cup orange, thin consistency

    1/4 cup purple, thin consistency

    1/4 cup pink, thin consistency

5 pastry bags and couplers

Decorating tips: round #2 and #3

1. Using a round tip #3, pipe red icing in a rectangle to form the outline of the front side of the dreidel and fill in the lines.

2. Using a round tip #3, pipe red icing to cover the triangle at the bottom of the dreidel. Let dry for 30 minutes.

3. Using a round tip #3, pipe yellow icing to cover the top of the dreidel.

4. Using a round tip #3, pipe orange icing to cover the right side of the dreidel.

5. Using a round tip #3, pipe purple icing for the stem of the dreidel. Let dry for 30 minutes.

6. Using a round tip #2, pipe a yellow outline around the whole cookie, except for the stem.

7. Using a round tip #2, pipe pink icing for the spiral on the face of the dreidel and for the outline and lines on the stem.

8. Using a round tip #2, pipe orange dots on the triangle at the bottom of the dreidel.

kids

What better project to enjoy with kids than baking and decorating cookies together? Decorate them, dip them in milk or hot cocoa, and enjoy!

TEDDY BEAR

(pattern page 118)

1 batch Butter Cookies

3 cups Royal Icing, divided and tinted with gel food coloring to make:

    2$\frac{1}{2}$ cups orange, thin consistency

    2 tablespoons green, thin consistency

    $\frac{1}{4}$ cup red, thin consistency

    2 tablespoons yellow, thin consistency

4 decorating bags and couplers

Decorating tips: round #2, #3, and #4

1. Using a round tip #3, pipe an orange outline around the cookie.

2. Using a round tip #4, pipe orange icing to cover the surface of the cookie up to the outline. Let dry for 10 minutes.

3. Using a round tip #3, pipe an orange outline on top of the first outline to create a bold border.

4. Using a round tip #3, pipe a large orange dot for the muzzle and a small dot for the belly button. Let dry for 30 minutes.

5. Using a round tip #2, pipe green dots for the eyes.

6. Using a round tip #2, pipe red icing for the mouth and the heart.

7. Using a round tip #2, pipe a yellow dot for the nose.

KID'S FACE

(pattern page 110)

1 batch Butter Cookies

3 cups Royal Icing, divided and tinted with gel food coloring to make:

  1½ cups off-white, thin consistency

  2 tablespoons blue, thin consistency

  ¼ cup red, thin consistency

  1 cup plus 2 tablespoons orange, stiff consistency

4 pastry bags and couplers

Decorating tips: round #2 and #4; open star #20

Paintbrush

Brown gel food coloring

1. Using a round tip #4, pipe an off-white outline around the cookie.

2. Using a round tip #4, pipe off-white icing to cover the surface of the cookie up to the outline. Let dry for 30 minutes.

3. Using a round tip #2, pipe blue dots for the eyes.

4. Using a round tip #2, pipe a red line for the mouth.

5. Using a round tip #2, pipe a large off-white dot for the nose and two more for the ears.

6. Using an open star tip #20, pipe orange icing for the hair. Let dry for 30 minutes.

7. Dip a paintbrush into brown gel food coloring and draw small lines for the eyebrows.

GINGERBREAD GIRL

(patterns page 118)

1 batch Gingerbread Cookies

3 cups Royal Icing, divided and tinted with gel food coloring to make:

    $1/2$ cup white, thin consistency

    2 cups yellow, thin consistency

    $1/2$ cup orange, thin consistency

3 pastry bags and couplers

Decorating tips: round #2, #3, and #4

1

Using a round tip #3, pipe a white outline around the head, hands, and feet.

2

Using a round tip #2, pipe white icing dots for the eyes and nose and a curved line for the smile.

3

Using a round tip #3, pipe a yellow outline in the shape of a skirt on the bottom part of the cookie.

4

Using a round tip #4, pipe yellow icing to cover the surface within the yellow outline. Let dry for 30 minutes.

5

Using a round tip #2, pipe orange dots on the skirt and a scalloped line at the bottom edge of the skirt.

flowers & fruit

Make any day of the year feel like spring with a bunch of strawberries and colorful flowers. Bring an assortment of cookie flowers instead of fresh ones the next time you're visiting friends.

BIG FLOWER

(pattern page 107)

1 batch Butter Cookies

3 cups Royal Icing, divided and tinted with gel food coloring to make:

    3/4 cup yellow, thin consistency

    1/2 cup light blue, thin consistency

    1 1/2 cups pink, thin consistency

    1/4 cup light green, thin consistency

4 pastry bags and couplers

Decorating tips: round #2, #3, and #4

1. Using a round tip #3, pipe a yellow outline around each petal of the flower. Let dry for 30 minutes.

2. Using a round tip #3, pipe light blue icing to cover the center of the flower. Let dry for 30 minutes.

3. Using a round tip #4, pipe pink icing to cover the surface of each petal up to the outline.

4. Using a round tip #2, pipe a light green spiral in the center of the flower.

STRAWBERRY

(pattern page 119)

1 batch Butter Cookies

3 cups Royal Icing, divided and tinted with gel food coloring to make:

    1 cup green, thin consistency

    1½ cups red, thin consistency

    ½ cup white, thin consistency

3 pastry bags and couplers

Decorating tips: round #2 and #3

1. Using a round tip #2, pipe green icing to cover the surface of the leaf. Let dry for 30 minutes.

2. Using a round tip #3, pipe red icing to cover the surface of the strawberry. Do not let the icing dry.

3. Immediately place the leaf at the top of the strawberry. The wet icing will glue the cookies together. Let dry for 30 minutes.

4. Using a round tip #2, pipe white dots all over the strawberry.

FLOWER ON A STICK

(pattern page 119)

1 batch Butter Cookies

3 cups Royal Icing, divided and tinted with gel food coloring to make:

$3/4$ cup orange, thin consistency

$1^1/2$ cups yellow, thin consistency

$3/4$ cup pink, thin consistency

3 pastry bags and couplers

Decorating tips: round #3

Popsicle sticks

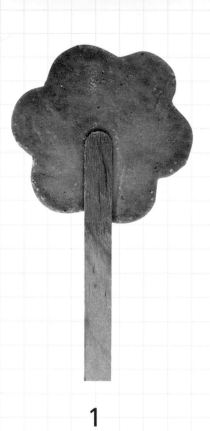

1

After cutting out the cookie shapes but before baking, press a popsicle stick into the bottom edge of each flower. Bake and cool as instructed, then place the cookies on the work surface with the popsicle stick side facing up.

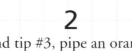

2
Using a round tip #3, pipe an orange outline around the center and petals of the flower. Let dry for 30 minutes.

4
Using a round tip #3, pipe pink icing to cover the center of the flower.

3
Using a round tip #3, pipe yellow icing to cover the surface of the petals. Let dry for 30 minutes.

bees & bugs

Here are some whimsical creature cookies that remind us of the beauty of nature.

BUTTERFLY

(pattern page 119)

1 batch Butter Cookies

3 cups Royal Icing, divided and tinted with gel food coloring to make:

    1/2 cup red, thin consistency

    1 3/4 cups orange, thin consistency

    1/4 cup pink, thin consistency

    1/2 cup yellow, thin consistency

4 pastry bags and couplers

Decorating tips: round #3

1. Using a round tip #3, pipe a red outline around the center of the cookie to form the body of the butterfly.

2. Using a round tip #3, pipe red icing to cover the surface of the body within the outline. Let dry for 30 minutes.

3. Using a round tip #3, pipe an orange outline around the body to create a bold border.

4. Using a round tip #3, pipe an orange outline around the wings.

5. Using a round tip #3, pipe orange icing to cover the surface of the wings. Let dry for 30 minutes.

6. Using a round tip #3, pipe a pink outline around the wings to create a bold border.

7. Using a round tip #3, pipe yellow decorations on the wings.

LADYBUG

(pattern page 119)

1 batch Butter Cookies

3 cups Royal Icing, divided and tinted with gel food coloring to make:

    1¹/₂ cups red, thin consistency

    1¹/₂ cups black, thin consistency

2 pastry bags and couplers

Decorating tips: round #3 and #4

1. Using a round tip #3, pipe a red outline around the wings.

2. Using a round tip #4, pipe red icing to cover the surface of the wings within the outline. Let dry for 30 minutes.

3. Using a round tip #3, pipe black icing to cover the round face and the wedge-shaped body between the wings. Let dry for 30 minutes.

4. Using a round tip #3, pipe black icing in slightly curved lines on top of the dry black icing on the body.

5. Using a round tip #3, pipe black dots on the red wings.

6. Using a round tip #3, pipe small black dots for the eyes.

BEE

(pattern page 120)

1 batch Butter Cookies

3 cups Royal Icing, divided and tinted with gel food coloring to make:

    2 cups yellow, thin consistency

    $5/8$ cup white, thin consistency

    6 tablespoons black, thin consistency

3 pastry bags and couplers

Decorating tips: round #3 and #4

1. Using a round tip #3, pipe a yellow outline around the oval body of the bee.

2. Using a round tip #4, pipe yellow icing to cover the surface of the cookie within the outline. Let dry for 30 minutes.

3. Using a round tip #3, pipe a white outline around the wings.

4. Using a round tip #4, pipe white icing to cover the surface of the wings. Let dry for 30 minutes.

5. Using a round tip #3, pipe a white outline on top of the first outline on the wings to create a bold border.

6. Using a round tip #3, pipe black horizontal lines on top of the yellow icing.

7. Using a round tip #3, pipe black dots for the eyes.

DRAGONFLY

(pattern page 120)

1 batch Butter Cookies

3 cups Royal Icing, divided and tinted with gel food coloring to make:

    1 cup light blue, thin consistency

    1 cup white, thin consistency

    $1/2$ cup green, thin consistency

    6 tablespoons blue, thin consistency

    2 tablespoons light green, thin consistency

5 pastry bags and couplers

Decorating tips: round #3 and #4

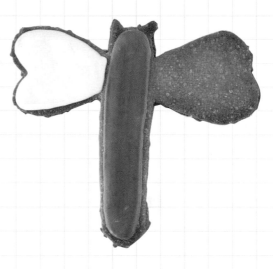

1

Using a round tip #3, pipe a light blue outline around the body of the dragonfly.

2

Using a round tip #4, pipe light blue icing to cover the surface of the cookie within the outline. Let dry for 30 minutes.

3

Using a round tip #3, pipe a white outline around the wings.

4

Using a round tip #4, pipe white icing to cover the surface of the wings. Let dry for 30 minutes.

5

Using a round tip #3, pipe blue lines across the body.

6

Using a round tip #3, pipe blue icing for the 2 lines representing the antennae.

7

Using a round tip #3, pipe green ovals on the wings.

8

Using a round tip #3, pipe light green icing around the green ovals on the wings to create a bold border.

sports

Why not treat those sports fans to fun cookies while they're watching the next game?

FOOTBALL

(pattern page 120)

1 batch Butter Cookies

3 cups Royal Icing, divided and tinted with gel food coloring to make:

    2^1/$_2$ cups brown, thin consistency

    ^{1}/$_2$ cup white, thin consistency

2 pastry bags and couplers

Decorating tips: round #1, #2, #3, and #4

1. Using a round tip #3, pipe a brown outline around the cookie.

2. Using a round tip #4, pipe brown icing to cover the surface of the cookie up to the outline. Let dry for 30 minutes.

3. Using a round tip #4, pipe white icing for the wide lines at the ends of the ball.

4. Using a round tip #2, pipe a brown outline on top of the first outline to create a bold border.

5. Using a round tip #1, pipe white icing for the line along the center of the ball. Let dry for 10 minutes.

6. Using a round tip #1, pipe white icing in short lines across the first line to represent the stitching.

BASEBALL SHIRT

(pattern page 109)

1 batch Butter Cookies

3 cups Royal Icing, divided and tinted with gel food coloring to make:

    2 cups white, thin consistency

    1 cup blue, thin consistency

2 pastry bags and couplers

Decorating tips: round #2, #3, and #4

1. Using a round tip #3, pipe a white outline to form the shape of the shirt.

2. Using a round tip #4, pipe white icing to cover the surface of the cookie up to the outline. Let dry for 30 minutes.

3. Using a round tip #2, pipe a blue outline around the edge of the shirt to create a bold border.

4. Using a round tip #2, pipe blue icing to double the border at the neck and sleeve openings.

5. Using a round tip #2, pipe blue icing in vertical lines on top of the white surface.

6. Using a round tip #2, pipe blue icing to form the shape and fill in the number in the center of the shirt.

SNEAKER

(pattern page 121)

1 batch Chocolate Cookies

3 cups Royal Icing, divided and tinted with gel food coloring to make:

    2 cups red, thin consistency

    1 cup white, thin consistency

2 pastry bags and couplers

Decorating tips: round #2, #3, and #4

1. Using a round tip #2, pipe a red outline around the sole of the shoe.

2. Using a round tip #4, pipe red icing to cover the surface of the sole within the outline. Let dry for 30 minutes.

3. Using a round tip #3, pipe a red outline around the upper sneaker shape.

4. Using a round tip #4, pipe red icing to cover the surface of the sneaker up to the outline. Let dry for 30 minutes.

5. Using a round tip #2, pipe white icing in thick and thin lines to represent the stripes, stitches, and laces.

BASEBALL

(pattern page 110)

1 batch Butter Cookies

3 cups Royal Icing, divided and tinted with gel food coloring to make:

    2½ cups white, thin consistency

    ½ cup red, thin consistency

2 pastry bags and couplers

Decorating tips: round #2 and #4

1. Using a round tip #4, pipe a white outline around the cookie.

2. Using a round tip #4, pipe white icing to cover the surface of the cookie up to the outline. Let dry for 30 minutes.

3. Using a round tip #2, pipe a white outline on top of the first layer to create a bold border.

4. Using a round tip #2, pipe white icing in two curving lines on each side of the ball.

5. Using a round tip #2, pipe red icing into little V shapes to represent the stitching along the curving white lines.

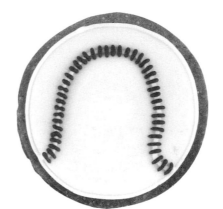

BASKETBALL

(pattern page 110)

1 batch Butter Cookies

3 cups Royal Icing, divided and tinted with gel food coloring to make:

    $2\frac{1}{2}$ cups orange, thin consistency

    $\frac{1}{2}$ cup black, thin consistency

2 pastry bags and couplers

Decorating tips: round #2, #3, and #4

1

Using a round tip #3, pipe an orange outline around the cookie.

2

Using a round tip #4, pipe orange icing to cover the surface of the cookie up to the outline. Let dry for 30 minutes.

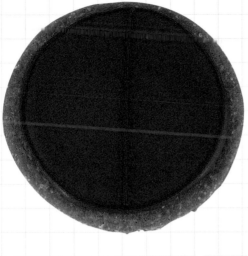

3

Using a round tip #2, pipe a black outline on top of the first layer to create a bold border.

4

Using a round tip #2, pipe a black vertical line from top to bottom down the center of the ball.

5

Using a round tip #2, pipe 2 curving black lines on either side of the vertical line. Let dry for 10 minutes.

6

Using a round tip #2, pipe orange dots all over the surface of the cookie.

fashion

For the fashion-conscious youngster or grown-up, here's something irresistible to add to the wardrobe.

HIGH HEEL

(pattern page 121)

1 batch Butter Cookies

3 cups Royal Icing, divided and tinted with gel food coloring to make:

   2½ cups purple, thin consistency

   ½ cup white, thin consistency

2 pastry bags and couplers

Decorating tips: round #2 and #3

1. Using a round tip #2, pipe a purple outline to form the shape of the shoe.

2. Using a round tip #3, pipe purple icing to cover the surface of the cookie up to the outline. Let dry for 30 minutes.

3. Using a round tip #2, pipe white dots to decorate the surface.

DRESS ON A STICK

(patterns page 121)

1 batch Butter Cookies

3 cups Royal Icing, divided and tinted with gel food coloring to make:

   2 1/2 cups light green, thin consistency

   1/2 cup pink, thin consistency

2 pastry bags and couplers

Decorating tips: round #2, #3, and #4

Popsicle sticks

1. After cutting out the cookie shapes but before baking, press a popsicle stick into the bottom edge of each cookie. Bake and cool as instructed, then place the cookies on the work surface with the popsicle stick side facing up.

2. Using a round tip #3, pipe a light green outline around the cookie, except for along the lower edge of the dress, leaving an 1/8-inch edge at the bottom.

3. Using a round tip #4, leaving the lower portion of the sleeves uncovered, pipe light green icing to cover the surface of the cookie up to the outline. Let dry for 30 minutes.

4. Using a round tip #2, pipe a light green outline on top of the first layer to create a bold border.

5. Using a round tip #3, pipe pink icing to cover the lower portion of the sleeves.

6. Using a round tip #2, pipe pink icing for the fringe on the lower edge of the dress.

PURSE

(pattern page 105)

1 batch Butter Cookies

3 cups Royal Icing, divided and tinted with gel food
coloring to make:

　1 cup pink, thin consistency

　1 cup yellow, thin consistency

　$2/3$ cup red, thin consistency

　$1/3$ cup light blue, thin consistency

4 pastry bags and couplers

Decorating tips: round #2, #3, and #4

Plastic straw

Narrow purple silk ribbons

1

After cutting out the cookie shapes but before
baking, use the straw to punch a small hole at
both ends on the top of the cookie, about $1/4$ inch
from the edge. Bake and cool as instructed.

2

Using a round tip #3, pipe a pink outline
around the bottom part of the cookie.

3

Using a round tip #4, pipe pink icing to cover
the surface of the cookie within the outline. Let
dry for 30 minutes.

4

Using a round tip #3, pipe yellow icing to cover the top part of the cookie. Let dry for 30 minutes.

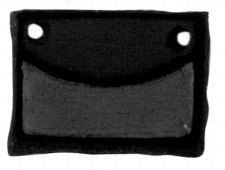

5

Using a round tip #2, pipe a red outline around the edge of the cookie and for the line between the top and bottom.

6

Using a round tip #2, pipe light blue lines to decorate the pink part of the cookie.

7

Using a round tip #2, pipe a light blue dot on the yellow icing to represent the snap.

8

Let the cookies dry for at least 12 hours.

9

Tie a purple silk ribbon through the holes before serving.

cookie
patterns

throughout this book we present all sorts of wonderful shapes for cookies—many more than you'll get with standard cookie cutters. Follow these easy steps to create the stencils for your cookie shapes and to cut out the dough.

1

Trace the cookie pattern with tracing paper and a pencil.

2

Cut out the pattern with a pair of scissors.

3

Place the pattern on a piece of thick cardboard and trace the shape with a pencil.

4

Using an X-acto knife or scissors, cut out the cardboard along the outline.

5

Place the stencil on top of your rolled-out dough and trace the shape with a knife.

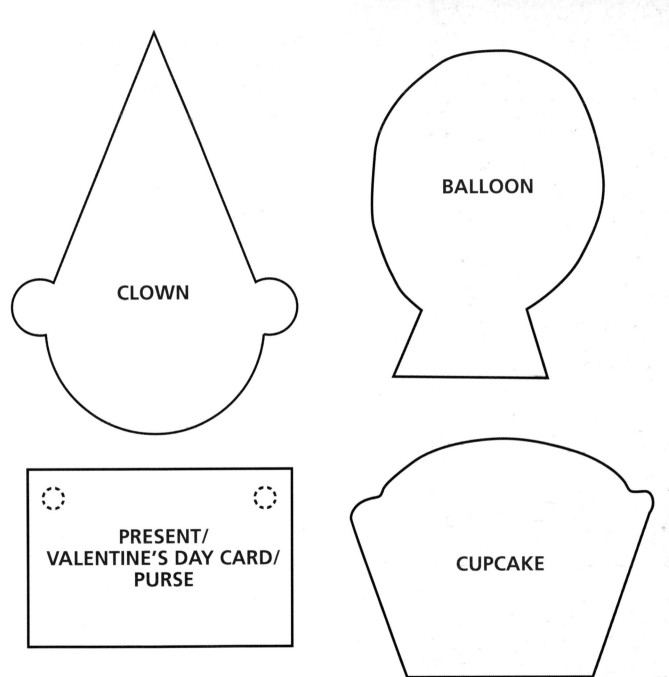

CLOWN

BALLOON

PRESENT/
VALENTINE'S DAY CARD/
PURSE

CUPCAKE

105

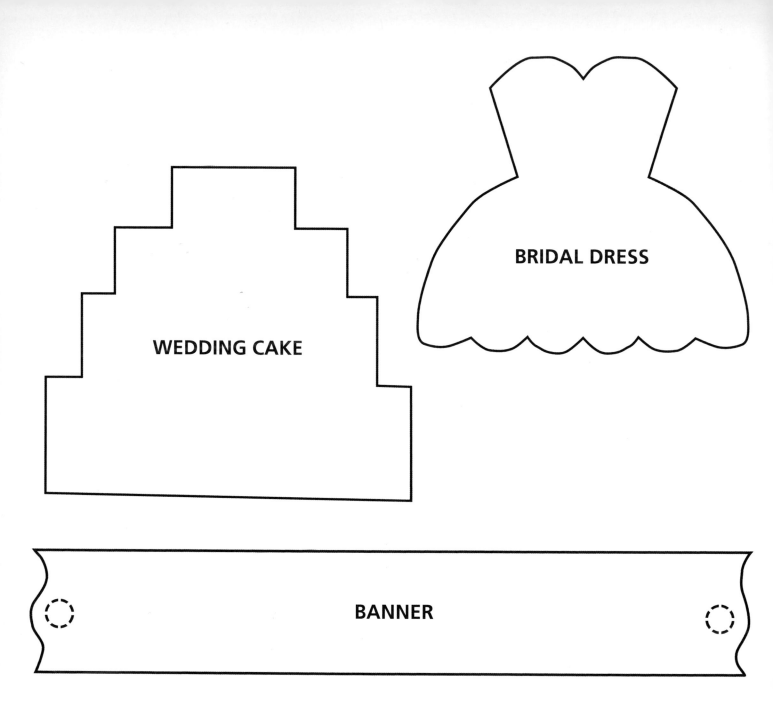

WEDDING CAKE

BRIDAL DRESS

BANNER

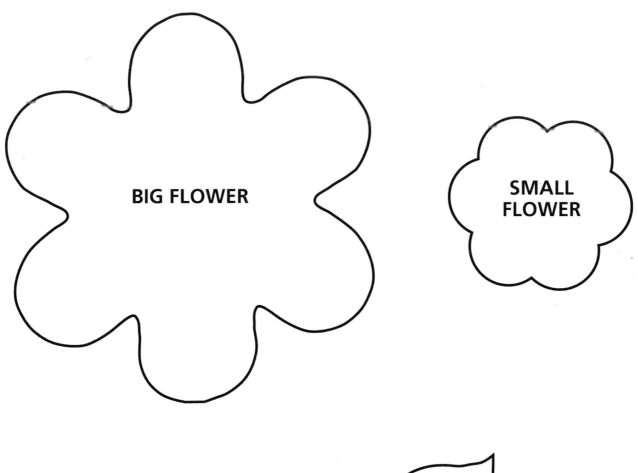

BIG FLOWER

SMALL FLOWER

LEAF

HEART

BABY BOTTLE

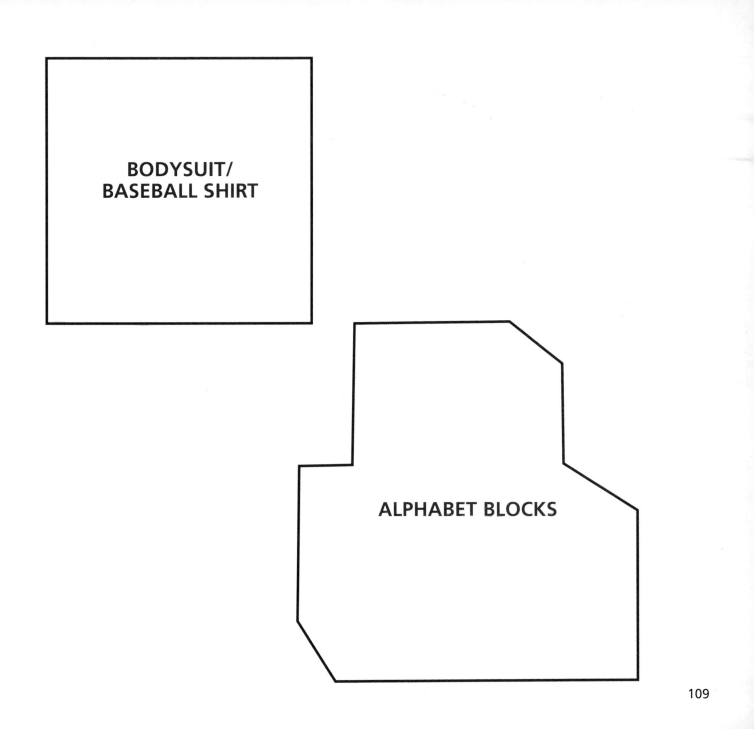

BODYSUIT/
BASEBALL SHIRT

ALPHABET BLOCKS

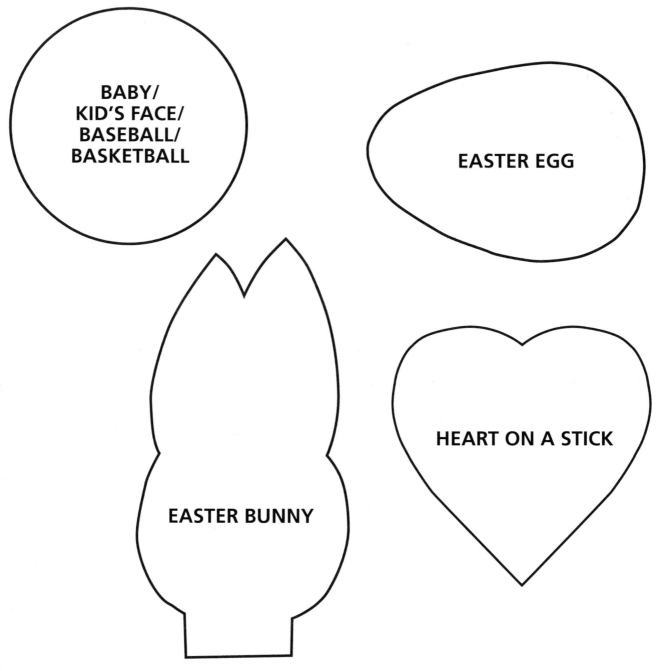

BABY/
KID'S FACE/
BASEBALL/
BASKETBALL

EASTER EGG

EASTER BUNNY

HEART ON A STICK

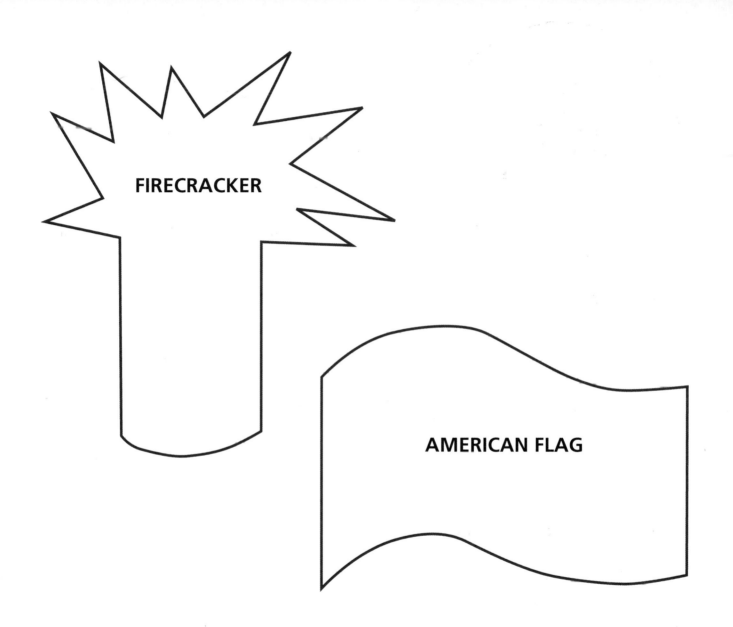

FIRECRACKER

AMERICAN FLAG

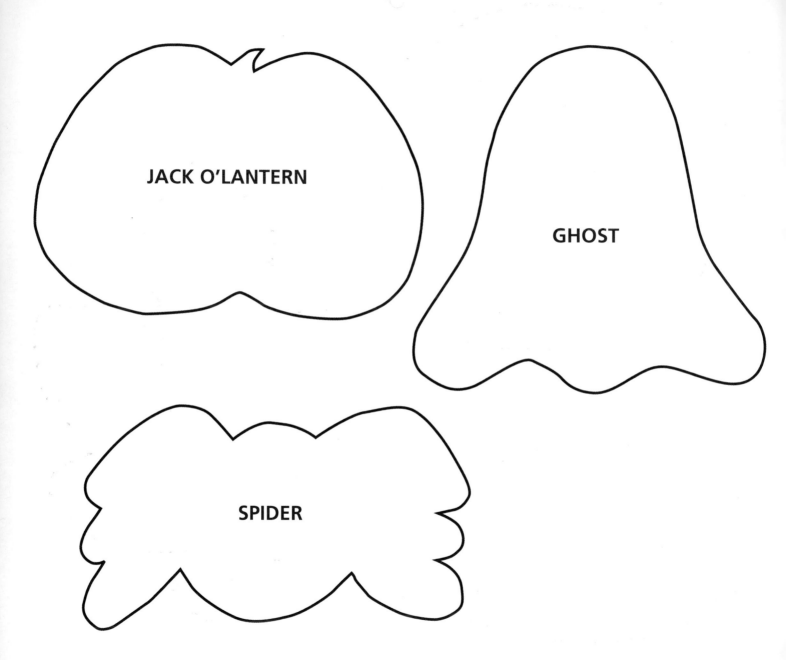

JACK O'LANTERN

GHOST

SPIDER

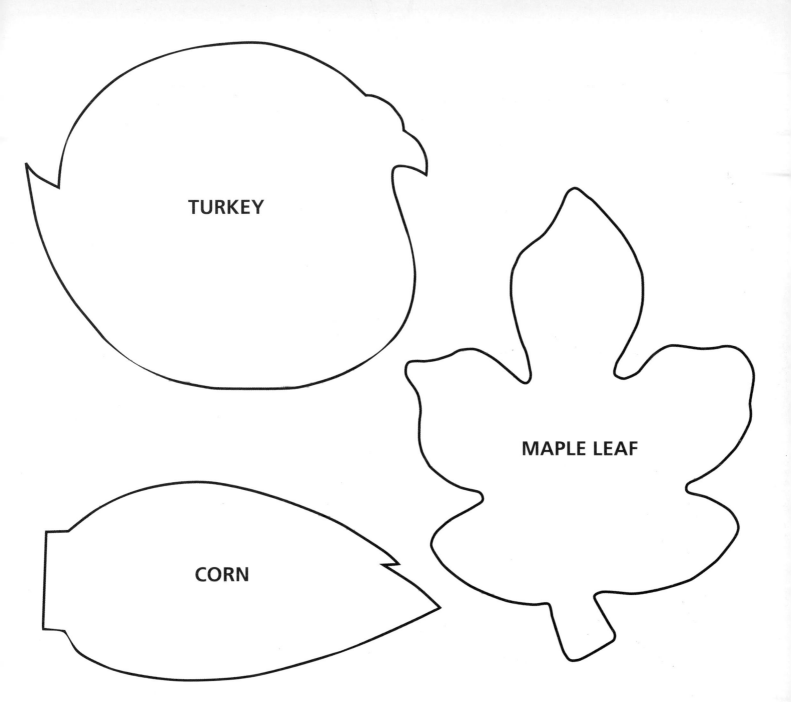

TURKEY

MAPLE LEAF

CORN

113

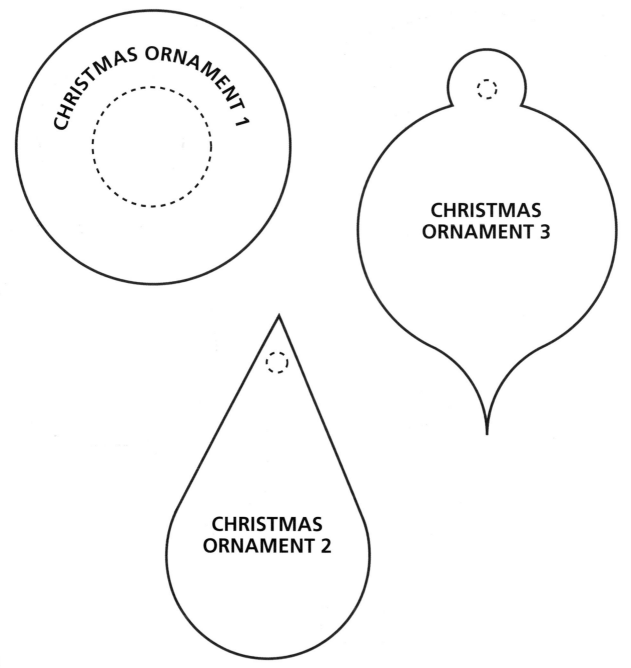

CHRISTMAS ORNAMENT 1

CHRISTMAS ORNAMENT 3

CHRISTMAS ORNAMENT 2

114

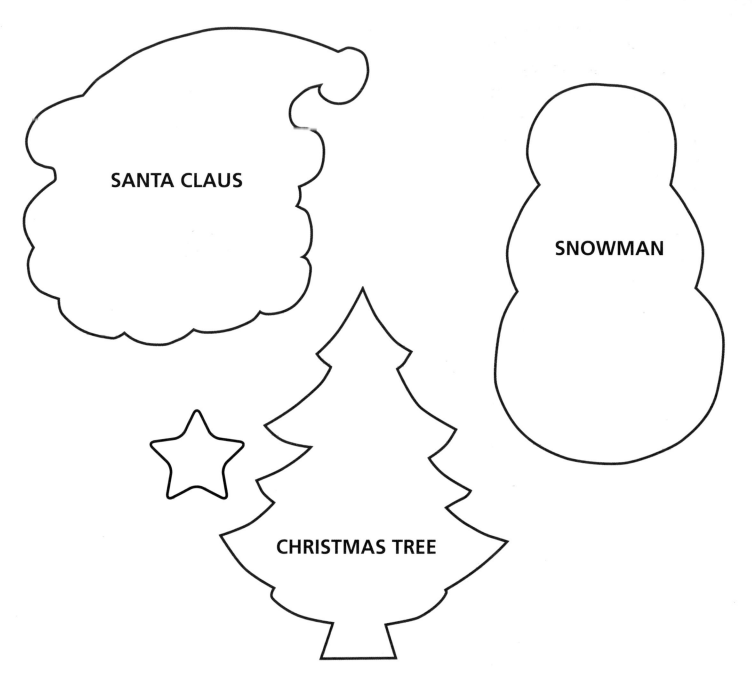

SANTA CLAUS

SNOWMAN

CHRISTMAS TREE

STAR

ANGEL

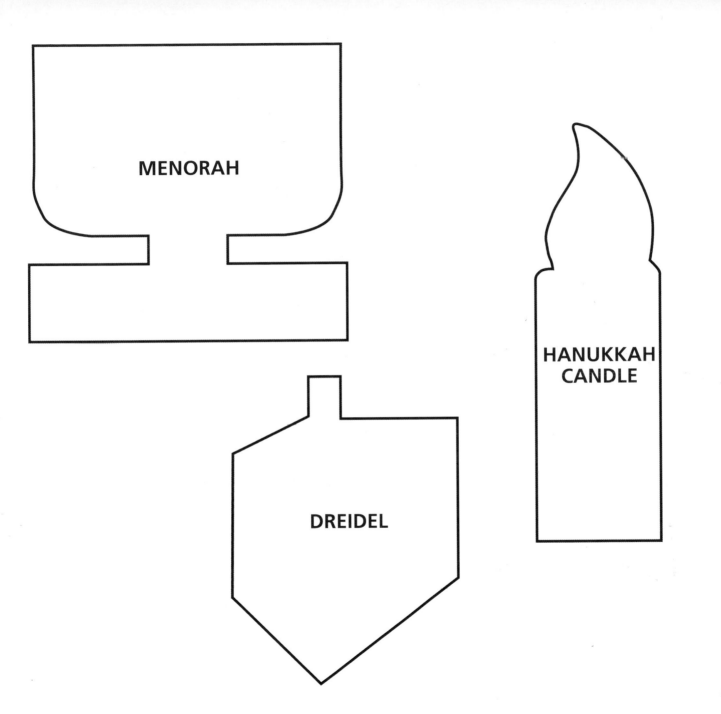

MENORAH

DREIDEL

HANUKKAH
CANDLE

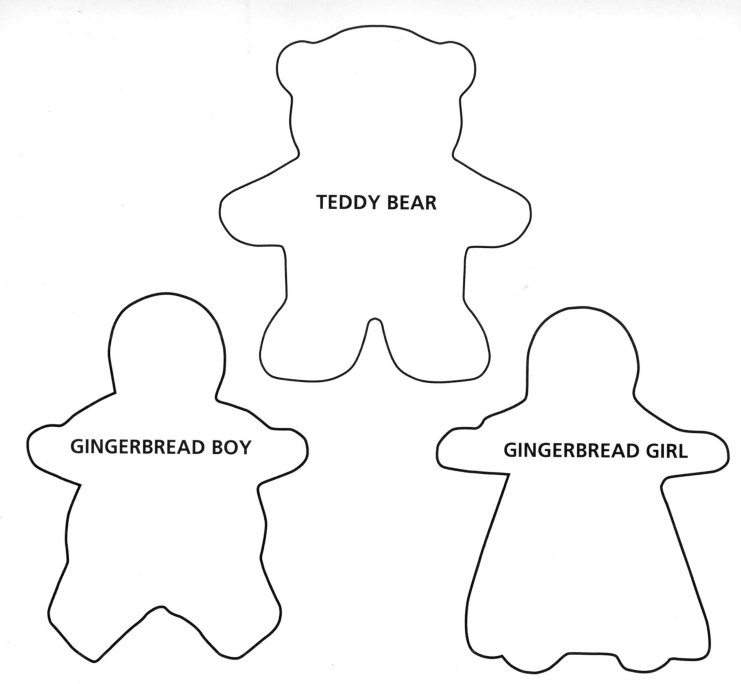

TEDDY BEAR

GINGERBREAD BOY

GINGERBREAD GIRL

118

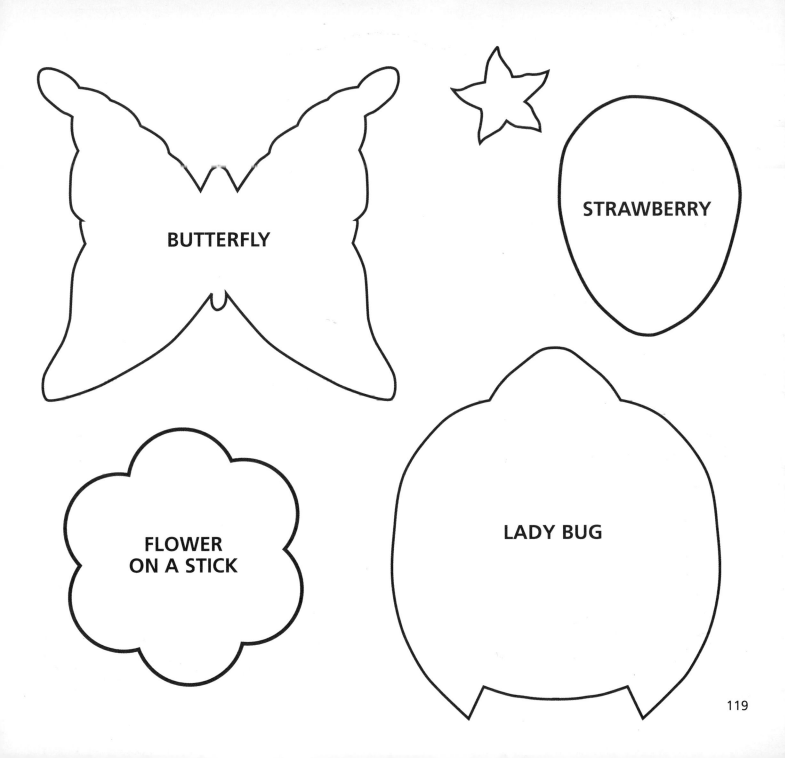

BUTTERFLY

STRAWBERRY

FLOWER
ON A STICK

LADY BUG

119

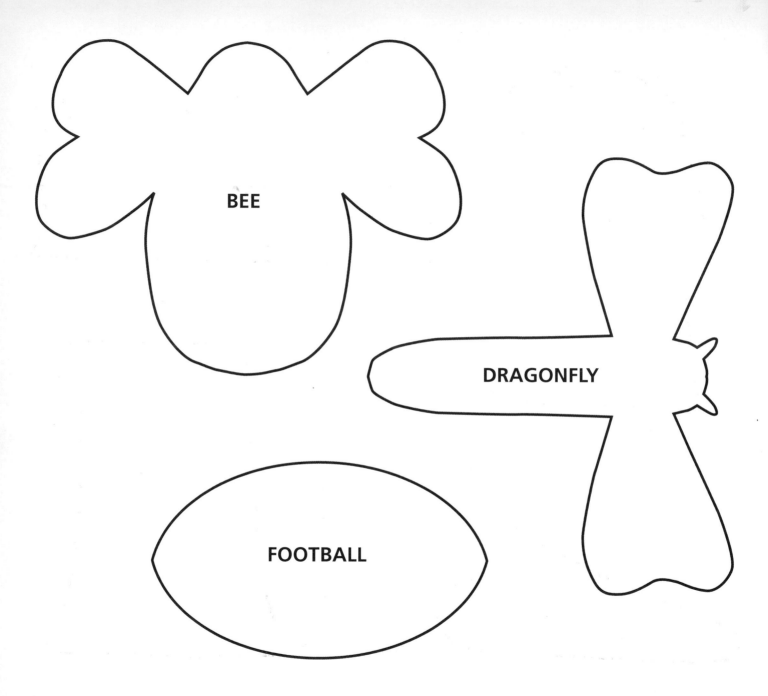

BEE

DRAGONFLY

FOOTBALL

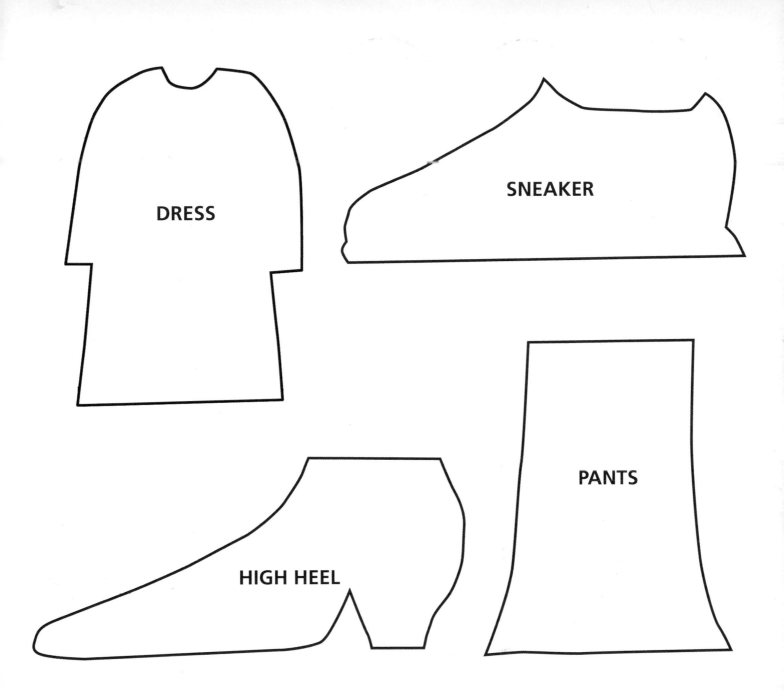

DRESS

SNEAKER

HIGH HEEL

PANTS